5/12/2015

INSTRUCTIONS
FOR THE
WISHING LIGHT

for Gary —
Former student, now a
POEMS friend.

with much affection,
Ann

ANN STALEY

booktrope

Booktrope Editions
Seattle, WA 2013

Cover Art by Judy Teufel

PRINT ISBN 978-1-62015-185-3

EPUB ISBN 978-1-62015-281-2

For further information regarding
permissions, please contact
info@booktrope.com.

for friend, colleague, poet, editor,
Jerri Otto

&

for my partner, counsel, tech support, humorist, love,
Courtney Cloyd

&

in memoriam
Claira Woolley
1924 – 2013

Claira was my dad's second wife, after my mother died (the first year I taught at PHS).

Contents

LIGHT

DO NOT FORGET WISHING

FRAGMENTED DREAMS & DAYDREAMS

INSTRUCTION

A KITE MINUS A STRING

CLOUDS IN A BLUE SKY

THE FIRE

LIGHT

ALL THIS TIME

The daffodils on the mantle began opening
after a few hours in tepid water.
The news itself takes longer, sometimes a decade,
for example the dam removal process.
But for murder it can be an immediately passionate moment
or come about after a lifetime of abuse.
In the oven this morning, it was 55 minutes for 350 degrees
for very crunchy mac and cheese,
And to gather together today's writing prompts,
an afternoon and two cups of tea.
While Rome burned, somebody fiddled,
While the ice floes melted, we argued science.
While the clouds piled-up along the Coast Range,
we began twenty-seven conversations.
All this time,
without the steady ticking of the Howard Clock,
we are inching toward spring,
crocus and violets responding to sunlight —
the earth's promise.

MAKING OUR WAY

From darkness
on a shadowed path,
I must make my way
—Shikibu

For anyone who grieves,
for anyone who is grieving today:
the friends and colleagues of the renowned
science teacher at Crescent Valley H.S.,
and for that 1,980th American soldier, age 20
from Niceville FL who was killed in Afghanistan yesterday,
and for someone who lost a younger sister,
and another whose beloved maiden aunt passed in Ohio.
Our world is filled with those leaving
and refilled by those arriving to take their places.

Across the way two women are discussing
Spring Light eco-friendly light bulbs.
A student reads a notebook of Xeroxed articles
neon yellow highlighter in hand,
a young father brings his infant son to lunch with a friend.

Amid the clink of coffee cups,
silverware sounds, murmuring voices,
it is a comfort beyond grief to be here at the cafe
on this cold, rainy afternoon,
traffic whooshing along 4th Street
heading north to the Bi-Mart or Albany,
commuters heading east to Lebanon and Interstate 5.
My friends breathe deeply, glance up, move their pens,
late-winter darkness coming on.

RHYMES WITH DAMMIT

What the river says, that is what I say.
—William Stafford

The Willamette dares the stranger
to say her name.
One needs the dictionary syllables —
wil am it' —
but even they are confusing.
The river says, "I have a direction,
and although I am racing now
after a January deluge,
I might meander in late August.
I have streamside beds and
the riverbed of the one-hundred-year flood,
a heron's nest at the bridge,
the inevitable otters.
You are welcome here
with your little dramas and sorrows.
You may sit and dream,
or speak to someone
in the Eastern Time Zone,
watch the walkers, the dogs on leashes,
the careening rebel skateboarders.
There is life here, an eternal flow,
one way toward the infinite."

PRAISE SONG IN FIVE STANZAS

After the Rose City adventure - three years in a condo,
anonymous sleeper with ear plugs,
with *Madame Butterfly*, Rembrandt and The Pearl,
I return to my sweet neighborhood and home
wondering about community, about the way paths
crisscross like 9th and Kings at 5 p.m.
circle like delirious and controversial roundabouts, or
maybe meander like Finley and Chip Ross trails.

At the library they still recognize me, at the Beanery too,
at the Arts Center, Grass Roots, and the Co-Op.
Tyee is the local winery, again, its hundred acres
held by Buchanans. And at the other end of town
Jackson and Frazier still flow through the Wetland,
birds chirping and swooping in December dusk.

The exuberant attorney, the PSN IVY specialist,
the psychologist, golf coach and geologist, are neighbors again.
College students, graduated to their next lives
leave stray cats, and make room for freshmen
parading in packs on Jefferson — heading downtown.
Jake is still recommending movies and music I'd never like,
and up at Withycombe a Playboy and Oedipus follow each other
just before the Bard hits the Quad as a musical
and quilts reappear all over town.

This town also welcomes flower baskets,
two days of outdoor farmers' bounty,
poems on the Midway Marquee, artisan bread, cheese and beer,
five cycle shops, and coffee never more than a few doors down.
Hidden-in-plain-sight-treasures, too,
a national journal of art and poetry,
the goings on at Shotpouch, the rose garden, the Greenbelt,
the Neighborhood Naturalist's birding bicycle tours.

Situated near the Willamette, Coast Range in sight,
there are luscious, Pacific-tinged sunsets, views of Marys Peak,
a riverside bicycle path all the way to Philomath
— and 42 inches of rain.
Down on the Riverfront, along with the bikers,
you can see the crows and the homeless,
joggers with strollers, skateboarders, chess players,
Free Speakers, and, sometimes,
a woman alone on a bench – writing.

PEONY NEBULA STAR

It rarely rains in the high desert of Central Oregon,
sustained heat and light making
for drought conditions and falling water-tables.
So it is no surprise that the few inhabitants of Baker County,
out beyond the crossroads hamlet named for the son of a Roman God,
enjoy nothing so much as a view of the cool night sky,
 that 180 degree dome of darkness,
speckled with the shimmering galactic white light of heaven.
Through a high-powered infrared telescope
a tiny group of writers on a spectacularly clear evening —
no fires, no moisture, no road dust or dust storm —
caught a once-in-a-million view
of the second brightest star in the Milky Way Galaxy:
White, orange and pink,
shaped like an irregular pupil, or a cell transforming,
like an amoeba trailing dust and light,
surrounded by a deeper darkness,
one massive star in the central region of our galaxy.

BEAGLES AND BORDER COLLIES

After the reading
she's got "the scent" of a fox,
and is practically howling for joy
as she describes the latest set of
circumstantial coincidences.
Her voice dances across the long-distance wire:
Ann, she says, you've got to check out this website,
hear the TED Lecture. It's all like the poems you read
and the message is: *If you want to tell your truth, be vulnerable.*

Later I follow her on-line directions
like the Border Collie I am.
I listen to the lecture:
Being able to give is a gift.
A gift requires taking note of something.
A gift lifts us beyond ourselves.
It's like hearing Rumi speak around a campfire,
flutes playing, everyone ready to dance.

Formal religions are incomplete,
They can't promise the holy light:
Aldous Huxley & I
and a whole flock of folks from Bloomsbury believe this.
Still I am drawn to the sacred, to what is marked by mystery.
Each of us carries an ordinary genius for something:
Like that Collie, my genius is herding words.

INSTRUCTIONS FOR THE WISHING LIGHT

—Wishing light rose slowly the sky
        do not forget wishing oh

This line is pure poetry, with a logic all its own.

The Dadaists did no better than the Chinese translator
for the Wishing Light.

Neither did Allen Ginsburg, howling his way through pages
of fragmented dreams and day-dreams.

This is assuredly the way I sounded speaking Portuguese
after six weeks of language instruction.

It's a fan with a blade missing, a kite minus a string,
a night light without the night or a bulb,

Georgia O'Keefe's eighty-foot long painting of clouds in a blue sky.
The fireside aquarium with the gold fish that has leapt into the fire.

PEPPERS IN GRAY LIGHT

—In response to a cover photograph from The SUN

It was a morning glimpse, really,
a moment in the long tumble of a week
that included riding the bus to work,
a phone call from the hospital,
you waving goodbye.
It was a week when the wind blew in from the Pacific
bringing winter torrents of rain & seven shades of gray
I memorized like a prayer.
Someone said, *Settling in is the essence of life.*
Someone said, *I wanted to protect.*
Someone asked, *Who will cry for the little girl?*
I thought about water, the calls of geese migrating north,
while I longed for the sound of my mother's voice.
And then in the early morning kitchen, gray holding on,
I saw the peppers, illuminated like a Montagna Madonna,
as beautiful, as holy—and my heart shifted one more time.

NIGHT WORDS

—For Courtney

Blue twilight —
I think of your gentle hands,
laughter.

At dusk
we pour red wine —
the fire crackles.

Western winds,
horizontal rain,
fir-fire smoke.

Nearly dark,
water drips from gutters,
leaves swirl along the bricks.

The sound of traffic on Jefferson,
your eyes reflect last light.

SEPTEMBER 11 REMEMBERED

The film with its dark music, the morning shadow
of the Statue of Liberty, stretching across water
a five-minute recounting, feels inevitable to our history now.
Startled awake on a clear September morning,
we supposed, at first, that some airplane had gone awry,
a pilot had a stroke, a mechanical error.
But twenty minutes later, when the second plane hit,
we knew something unspeakable had happened,
some new peril appeared from nowhere.
A continent away, I felt a deep bifurcation of my heart,
this event, unimaginable — a Hollywood movie.
All morning while Courtney attended a conference,
I watched the TV reruns of thirty devastating minutes —
people jumping from the burning buildings,
the collapse of the towers,
pedestrians running from a cloud of smoke and debris.
Then I drove across the valley to a friend's house
where we watched, again in silence.
Outside September blazed on, bright and indifferent
to the days and months ahead:
could there be a nuanced response, I wondered
shocked and loyal, the nations of the world stood with us.
At the time I hoped our leaders would breathe and pray.
I hoped for wisdom without revenge.

ALL-AMERICAN SONNET

—written in good company

The babes, the beer, the National Anthem shouted off-key.
Oh say can you see — Brock, Spencer, Braxton, and Jace.
It's the Papa's Pizza "to go" inning, dough for dough.

Steven played for the Fabulous Flamingos; Jackson for the
      Geezers,
Courtney for the Peerless Rooms One-Eyed Cats.
Susan, not a believer, still played for the First Presbyterians.

Brooks wrestled for the Golden Gophers; Ann starred for the Indians,
Rita danced for the Orcasus "Rite of Spring."
Bottom of the 3rd, homerun for O'Neill, Number 4, from Tracey CA.

After the hot-dog-run, the score stands 2-1, East All Stars ahead.
We heard the fans from CH2MHill, but not a single Philomath
      Rotarian.
While standing for that Seventh Inning Stretch, and after singing

Take Me Out To The Ball Game, the sun sets, the fireworks commence,
the Union Pacific slides through our sleepy town.

MEADOW

Meadow is spring.   Is green.   Grasses, Dandelion, Larkspur, Buttercup, leaves reaching toward sunlight.   Apple blossoms disintegrate to the sound of water over rock.   The bees.   The sunset.   The 27 shades of green my friend counted a few years ago. You are silent.   I am singing.   Still.   That blessed buzz of joy. Remembering.   Dreaming.   This song isn't Lennon.   It's the blues at dusk, Etta singing.   Some saxophone rant.   Meadow of sorrow. Of sound.   The song.   The sky.   Stars appearing above the grasses.

Wishing Light rose slowly the sky
do not forget wishing oh

DO NOT FORGET WISHING

POET IN A TIME OF WAR

—For the soldiers, for the peace-makers

This is what we're doing, isn't it?
Ignoring the generals and their advisors,
substituting fresh asparagus for drones.
We've gathered to write and share,
a small circle encircled by other circles.
In this town, Veterans for Peace &
the National Guard unit returned from a thirteen-month deployment.
In this town, those planning a festival,
those filling care packages—cigarettes, cookies, socks—for the troops.
I applaud our presence-with-opposing-views—without guns.
This is what our country stands for.
Not big business, not corporations as persons, not big oil and gas.
We bend our heads as though in prayer—*in* prayer.
We make our thinking visible on the page
our memories, hopes and desires visible.
Silence and words create this sacred place
where we know and can be known,
in a time of war.

STONE HARBOR, 1950

Hair, dark and wet
from warm Atlantic water,
now shivering from sun-burn and dehydration
I am wrapped in a white, terry-cloth robe,
    initials monogrammed in red.
Here is a lineman's stance before bending
    for the snap and tackle.
the stance of a sister with an older
    tormenting brother.

When I turn thirteen, girls effect new roles:
    demure, coy, and cute.
I consider the Convent
or a life without love.
I want to be a boy!

Decades later, I still feel this bold girl,
    smart and bossy,
who out-ran some of the boys
and all of the girls.

SISTER

I always wanted one.
More than the pony or piano lessons
I added to my mother's shopping list the year I was twelve.
I considered becoming one, too – Sister Theresa Ann –
and was one
to an older and younger brother,
the rose between two thorns
my mother used to say,
kidding those boys she loved so.
I was wanted. She made that clear,
and named for a great-great grandmother
so we could hang her portrait
above the living room mantle.
I didn't just want a sister, I've sought them as well.
Always.
A bevy of best friends from Ruthie Feiser onward:
Betty, Debby, Judy, Cynthia, Debbie, Sandy, Mary Louise, Patti.
Kathy, Florence, Joan, Cindy, Beth, Karen, and Jerri.
A flock of feminists
four writing circles
one book club
numerous correspondents
former students, all grown up now,
mentors and bosses
women I barely knew
women I didn't know at all.
Sandra Day O'Connor — who cared that she was a Republican!
When she was announced I wept in the Student Memorial Union.
Wilma Mankiller, Cindy Sheehan, Steinem
Emily Carr, Judy Chicago, O'Keefe,
Austen, Evans, Woolf,
Mary Oliver, Emily, Jane Kenyon.
At the moment I'm losing one of my dearest friends
as another is stepping over the wide water I created as a defense.

The sisters believe and act and do,
Carolyn down at the courthouse every evening
for the years we've been in Afghanistan –
one more grandmother for peace.
This afternoon I visit with Be
and plan a celebration for the Autumn Equinox.
I keep track of my life with *The Women Artists Datebook,*
which quotes Virginia Woolf this week:
Arrange whatever pieces come your way, to which I add,
Sister!

MRS. KITCHEN

Teaching is about making 400 close-judgment calls a day.
—Wise-Teacher comment

...traveled the world with her M.D. husband,
both working for the American Red Cross.
They returned to suburban Harrisburg
and began the next chapter of their lives.
Mrs. Kitchen became a 2nd grade teacher
at Progress Elementary School.
Our classrooms had floor-to-ceiling windows,
which opened so you could hear recess voices,
and dark wooden floors polished to a sheen.
We were seated, not in the usual rows,
but in a square "u" of desks.
We were allowed to sit with whomever
we wanted, as long as our work was uninterrupted
by giggling (the girls) or hitting (the boys).
Mrs. Kitchen was small in stature, big in heart.

She wore glasses and had curly brown hair.
She loved all her students, but had,
I realized even then, a soft spot for me.
I didn't understand why and still don't.
Every afternoon, in the hour before school ended,
she read aloud to us – from books
on The New York Times Bestseller list.
Kon Tiki is one I remember most vividly.

Winifred Kitchen taught "up" to us,
believing that eight-year-olds could understand more
than the 1950's psychology books expected.
This was her great gift to her fortunate students.
We studied Cro-Magnon and Neanderthal men,
then made shadow boxes depicting their lives.

One day when I'd finished my work early,
she sent me to the library, alone, saying,
Get whatever book you want, Ann.
That day I chose a book titled *The Pigtailed Pioneer,*
about a girl whose covered wagon arrives in Portland, Oregon,
where she meets her first Indian in an encampment south of town.
I had braids, then, which my mother plaited each morning,
tying on plaid or satin ribbons that she ironed.
Girls still wore dresses to school in those days,
no pants allowed until we got to Junior High School.
Jeans – never!

One afternoon I asked Mrs. K. if I could go to the office
without being sent there. I wanted to meet the principal,
a woman, but wanted to go there on good terms.
She arranged an interview with this imposing woman.
After we finished speaking, the Principal told me to
sit behind her desk, answer the phone if it rang.
She was going out for her usual late afternoon of listening
to the classrooms with open doors. I was thrilled.
My 2nd grade year convinced me that I wanted to be a teacher.
I set up summer school for my dolls in the basement
and began, in earnest, my professional life.

DRIVE FROM CORVALLIS

Highway 99 North
green like June
fields of hops
agricultural workers gathered
around a large tractor,
some fields newly turned,
not much traffic.
Listening to Ray Charles,
Ray and Van Morrison,
Ray and Johnny Mathis,
Ray and KD Laing,
Ray and me.
I join in, sipping coffee
belting it out
like the soul I hope to be
next time around.

FAR FROM HOME

A place far from home.
It was never what you'd imagine,
more like a crow flying out of left field
as he listens to the news.

I carried my loneliness like a thorn,
what I felt but could not name.
I passed near the animal's lair,
that place in the grasses where

I could see they'd bedded down all spring,
borne and suckled their young.
Call it what you will — the roots were visible
leaf layered upon leaf.

I'd call it a safe-haven for the innocent,
a place far from home.

LETTER TO SR:

I missed, entirely,
the chance
to write with you,
say *Adios*.
However, because
it's only 8:24
and Frontline
doesn't come on
until 10,
and because
the moon is full
{in both
hemispheres?}
and because
Georgia O'Keefe
said,
I've been absolutely
terrified every moment
of my life,
I just want to
say that I
haven't been
terrified.
Only a few
times of terror,
but much more
joy.
A fortunate one,
I know,
but then, too,
sometimes
not.

Which is to say
I've been
heart-broken
and just plain
broken,
but still I
talk to strangers
at the PO
and give money
to the homeless
men along
the river.
It's very cold
here, starry sky
and that moon,
and I'm
imagining you
with the house repairs
and the warmth
and the books
and the walking.
Love to you
from just below
the 45th parallel.

RECREATIONAL MATHEMATICS

—*With thanks to Steve Wilson*

Count the black tiles on the kitchen floor
the stairs stepping downward
to your basement on Penbrook Avenue.
Count the stacked firewood,
how many fires remain?
Don't try for the pear blossoms,
but go ahead and count the dead branches
to be removed from the Japanese Maple
caught out in the too-cold January nights.
Measure the distance your heart must travel
to Resurrection Cemetery,
all you've been unable to share with the friend
who wrote, *Have a nice life.*
Compute whatever you can make
of last night's dream, including
your first husband and his sweet dog, Ned.
Chart the miles to Tampa, to Tulsa, to Ithaca,
places where lost things have been found.
Codify what silence absences have filled.
Chart your next drive to the ocean,
too cold to step into, too beautiful to ignore.
Finally, find the value of d, that fourth side
of the quadrangle of which you are a part.

SONNET IN TWELVE LINES

The river is at flood stage,
the east bank giving way to the golf course and pasture land.
The river walk and bike path are inaccessible,
that spot where I phoned the Central Time Zone,
drowned like our relationship.

In the coffee shop four women talk with a soldier in camouflage.
Three men work on their laptops at separate tables,
two women discuss fund-raising for charity,
one mom watches her daughter in a polka-dot dress.
The Viet Nam Vet observes in rare silence.

There's not water enough to stop the 4th Street traffic,
nor enough to staunch this grief.

SOLACE

What cannot be said will be wept.
—Sappho

To be here is solace.
The sweet, cool afternoon breeze
floats up from the creek,
cools the deck where I sit in shade,
where Jenny is stretched-out,
where the Dictionary is closed,
where my heart, carrying both
        love and sorrow,
accepts both burdens,
and the fact that both sorrow and love
are tied together like a perfect square knot
on a boat shoe or a Cole Haan dress shoe.

In this place the knot loosens,
one may walk barefoot
even as the bees buzz,
knock themselves silly
trying to penetrate plate-glass,
where a moth, brown with a rust-colored sheen
dances above September's golden grasses
then disappears.

I don't know how much
my human heart can hold,
but I want to hold this moment:
the shade, the water sounds,
in the breast pocket of my work shirt,
        near my heart.

SPIRIT GUIDE

They say we have them,
angels and protectors,
saints we're named for,
whose story we might strive to imitate.
My father told my step-mom
there were angels
at the bottom of his Hospice bed,
and I hoped this was true.
His death was a slow agony;
he stopped eating,
I spoke long-distance
to him an hour before he died,
he squeezed Claira's hand.
I have no sense
that my protecting angel is present.
Things seem more like luck, chance,
a roll of the dice,
though one time I did hear an angel presence,
Alice Walker,
who appeared above the mountains
in Eastern Oregon while I was driving
to a conference in Boise.
Keep on writing, she said.

GRATITUDE

for the New Year
bright sky, bitter cold,
for relentless rain
and Pacific winds,
the Jet Stream west of the coast
that sets it all in motion,
for the fog nurturing Sitka Spruce,
the downhill gradient moving the creek along,
for the cabin Franz built and donated to us all,
for brass knobs that turn
and glass pulls,
for tea lights by the 100's,
for the political spectrum,
for friends who no longer like me,
for praise & forgiveness
and wounds that heal,
for the healers,
for the unexpected, arriving out of left field,
the grounder the short-stop misses,
the home run.
For bicycles, for whomever invented them
and fire when necessary.
For the strength abandonment teaches,
for loyalty deserved and otherwise,
for the surety of instinct
and passion rekindled.
For songs sung in moving cars
and old books sent by mail.
For parents and children doing their best,
brothers and sisters — cousins too.
For the special aunt, the grandmother who knits
and neighbors who care.
For sinner and saint,
the black sheep

and the little black dress.
For golf course landscapes
and sunsets when the new Titleist is lost forever.
For desks and the silence that surrounds them.
For the chorus from the bookshelf,
cats and dogs
and birds in flight.
For the neighing pastured mare
and the corn field which she longs to graze.
For the twenty-one lichen that purify our air
and gravel roads in winter.
For the post office sending our messages along,
for beautiful stamps on letters hand-addressed.
For gin and tonic
the limes, too.
For the historian, the poet, the choir director,
the believer in dreams.
For basil pesto, warm garlic bread,
for winter & three kind words.
For a God we're questioning, counting on,
and the goddesses waiting offstage.
For blossoming cherry trees, for the Sweet Gum,
for empty notebooks awaiting words,
for music dreamed at night,
the artist's first show,
the off-off-Broadway musical.
For the architect's plan,
the actor memorizing her lines
and the nuclear engineer teaching composition.
For leaders, counselors, lawyers,
who must both listen and hear.
For safety guards, E-room nurses, first responders.
For your favorite teacher and the substitute,
and those who watch in darkness
to bring the planes safely down.
For the soldier missing home
and those who await him,

for a traveler stepping into the unknown.
For the new-born, the elders,
the wisdom of innocence & experience.
For every new friend we make,
and the old friends who remember us.
For reunions of every kind,
your dearest love, the kindly heart.
For joy,
hopefulness,
the holy beginning
and its sacred end.

The Dadaists did no better than the Chinese translator for the Wishing Light. Neither did Allen Ginsberg howling his way through pages of fragmented dreams and daydreams.

FRAGMENTED DREAMS AND DAYDREAMS

TALKING WITH THE DEAD

The mystics say you are as close as my own breath, and it is obvious that if I want to complete this sentence I must breathe, let that exhale escape into the presence of a cedar grove that stands as witness here, so I breathe and hear birdsong more insistent than traffic, as sunny as this October afternoon.

I feel I am always talking with you, Tom, lost to the streets many years ago. I haven't read your letters from the months before you died or my flimsy answers, sent along with every hope that was inside me then. Still, we talk as I pass by the homeless man who sleeps on the steps of the First Christian Church, and when I give to any one of these lonely souls I say, *If there's a sister, mother, or aunt in your life, call her, let her know you're alive.*

I pack the Limoges to send back across the continent to my cousin's grown-up daughter. I remember the day it arrived on the west coast, each cup, plate, platter wrapped by my mother and Aunt Anne and sent to fill the china cupboards of our new home. *You'll be happy to know, Mom, that the china is now relocated on the east coast with Betsy Anne's only daughter, Cindy. She manages a bookstore and lives alone with her dog, a bright and independent young woman.*

I have things to say to the dead, whether I breathe or not, on-going conversations, news from this side of the veil.

ANOTHER LAUNDROMAT STORY

What do you know about physics, he asked. My answer, *Nothing,* didn't matter in the least. He went on to talk about the recent Nobel Laureates in Physics and their theories refuting quantum mechanics & about a trio of them who predicted a one-atom-thick graphene object in space that has since been located and photographed by the Spitzer Telescope, the very same one that photographed the Peony Nebula I was asking my friend, Jim, about a couple of days ago. This stranger smelled a little when he got close, the smell of someone who hasn't showered recently, gesticulating, maybe ranting. When he loaded his laundry into the dryers, there was no sorting, just a jumble of colors and textures and ten minutes on high for each.

I like to go to the laundromat for just these kinds of encounters, though this man seemed on-edge. I believe my pupils were dilated when I walked outside to the car. Plus, I had to return after a meeting to get my things from the dryer. I hoped he wouldn't be there, that is, I hoped he didn't do folding.

DREAMS AND DAYDREAMS

1.
The postcard from New York City — a former student
enjoying a day without her children.
The travel mug returned to the back door step,
and the tidy stack of cedar fence rails.
The herb garden, earth turned, rosemary planted.
An email written at 4:15 a.m., *Are you coming for coffee?*
The greeter's smile in the Administration Building,
the joke made as we pass through the metal detector.
These everyday gestures, given freely, without thought,
these narrow bands of sunlight are also called love.

2.
After this day, there will be an empty page,
a bowl waiting to be filled.
A large yellow bowl, like the one my Nana used
to mix the ingredients for Hot Cross Buns.
In the yellow bowl of tomorrow, I want another cup of coffee,
the next chapter in *The Haiku Apprentice*, the answer to how
Obama might win the Presidency. I want leek and potato soup,
chives sprinkled on top, and the final episode of *West Wing.*

3.
It's Wednesday and chalky light seeps through the curtains.
Interrupted sleep, dreams almost as empty as the cat's bowl,
almost as lonely. Exhausted after an evening drive from Newport
over the Coast Range with snow and fog,
Election news unstoppable on the radio, headlined front-page
announcements. All that was written yesterday, those words
pouring out, where I'm from, where I'm going, baffle me —
join the river that is this notebook.
Coffee. Scone. Light changing. It's midway through
the first week of February. I have somewhere to go.

IMAGINE

—With thanks to Robert Bly, Things To Think

Think in a new way, Ann,
    relying on the left side of your brain.
If the phone rings, imagine
    that when you pick it up,
a brass band will begin with *76 Trombones*
    and end with *Ode to Joy*.

Think that an owl has risen from the day-lit lake,
    carrying in his talons,
a Valentine mailed in 1957.
    Think that a stranger might deliver a pony
to the kitchen door,
    maybe a pinto or a dappled gray.

When someone knocks,
    think it is your mother
returned from the Elsewhere to forgive you,
    to say she's proud of who you've become,
and she's decided that it's okay to give away
    the family antiques to chosen friends.

When the dream with the blue door reappears,
    think about a deep pool of water,
looking from below to the surface light.
    Or consider this heaven
where the soul floats in solitary contentment,
    the Earth seen from deep space.

CHILDHOOD MUSIC

—*After Galway Kinnell*

Didn't the stars sing at night then, blazing above the cornfields at Madars? And those three birches in constant conversation at the west corner of the lawn. Mica shimmered in granite, whispering when you walked past, noticing. In the ravine, wild violets, an early summer swath, like the Latin Mass when it was the only sanctioned version. And your mother's voice, with the timbre of wide-brimmed hats and cigarettes, returns in a dream decades after her death. If your grandfather phoned now, you'd never have to say, *Who is calling*? You doubt you'd recognize any beloved classmate's voice, although you did then. At night you listened to the radio in darkness, in the room shared with your older brother, his voice remembered even after a silence of many years. Nana's knitting needles, the Singer zipping along in the basement sewing room, the sound of skates on cement, the casement windows cranked open in any room of our corner ranch house. A screen door slamming shut in summer, typing along on an Underwood – slow, leaden, plunk-plunk, plunk. The bright "ding" when it was time to return the carriage. The silverware I dried after dinner dropping into the felt-covered chest. Opening the kitchen junk drawer, where flotsam and jetsam mixed with tacks, bands, coupons. You poke around and maybe find what you need.

We had a portable record player for the children, and some story records, narratives sung by chipmunks or Danny Kaye. These, followed by a collection of twenty classic Classical LPs, where I learned to love "The Unfinished Symphony"—Romantic, like the books I read then, the dreams I had. A snow shovel scraping brick on a winter morning, the softened sounds of cars, milk bottles left at the back door, the ring of our black rotary phone, 545-3250 for the decades we lived in Green Acres. Wind in the side-yard pines we planted. *Didn't the stars sing at night then?*

NOTES TO SELF

It's January, the month of malaise.
On my desk, letters wait for words to equal them.

I know so little and that little learned by leaving.
All maps are somehow flawed.

It's not much fun to be older unless you have a granddaughter.
Why aren't you writing?

Today I feel as deep as dust, as insightful as grass.
Why is this journal going on and on?

When I move my pen along, it's just me breathing,
breathing again, words on empty lines, necessary and
    inconsequential.

In the dream, I was being prevented
from seeing someone I wanted to see.

The satisfactions of agreement are as immediate as sugar.
Literacy floats on a sea of talk.

In our quiet, empty living room, the candles glow.
Mystics believe it takes years for sorrow to reach the soul.

We are always carrying an invisible grief and,
Bill Stafford would say, *our one little fire.*

Obsidian and pumice have identical chemistry.
We are all like pebbles.

I fell in love with Edith Piaf so I learned French.
It's easy to begin. Let us recognize all kinds of memory.

When I look back, a whole day reappears.
The past is not dead, it's not even past.

ARRIVAL

Imagine
Paris, not Texas
but the one along the Seine,
a twilit, cloud-covered sky
streaks of cool light along the horizon,
a Ferris Wheel with forty covered chairs.
City lights sparkle like downed stars,
two lamp posts make, of you, a shadow.
You've arrived by train,
by cab,
by thumb
with the leather duffel
that belonged to your Dad.
No one in the world knows where you are tonight,
alone,
arriving.

SHE CANNOT SAY

That tension you feel. Did I create it or is it actually there?
a bald man wearing black high-tops asks across the table.

Nearby, Johnny Cash sings, a woman sweeps the floor,
the wall clock's hour numerals lie in a pile between 6 and 7.

In the next room, a series of landscapes suggest days
unlike this one, Pacific Northwest gray and wet.

What spirits dwell where breakfast is served all day?
The muses and the one William Stafford met, too.

The geologist knows the why of rocks and sand, the mountains.
I'm firmly planted in the Now.

We meet at twilight over a glass of wine, light candles,
feel only gratitude — how lucky we are.

Close of March, the ending goes on and on. What has been lost
will never return — a blessing, fate, a bit of unavoidable bad luck.

LIFE STORY

When I lived in the red brick house,
life inside looked secure and perfect,
but I knew there was more:
complexity, anger, passion.

In the State College apartment, before Senior year,
I had no idea about the loss sneaking up on me
like the surprise hurricane that hit
the summer I was eight.

I had a repetitive dream, then, about
placing a bomb at the top of a building,
then running, throwing myself on the ground,
to be clear of the explosion.

Earlier there was a summer of wild violets.
The boy I loved then
was playing around in that same ravine
with bows and arrows.

I felt no brimming happiness in my early life,
not until I discovered it in friendship,
but I was happy enough.
Later I found that kind of happiness in love.

I knew, or thought I did, how to "read" people.
When I picked-up hitchhikers that summer I drove west,
they told me their secrets
but didn't ask about mine.

In Oregon at 25 I began to understand why,
to see the ways I kept control —
a good thing when you teach adolescents,
a bad thing in relationships.

Finally, I wanted to escape *control*
and discovered that it
was only a cover —
for loneliness & vulnerability.

Now I am here,
pen moving along these blue lines.

OTHER ROADS, OTHER STORIES

Her mother divorces her father in 1950. Then what?
The violin or ice skates sustain her.

She misses Foreign Film Night, goes swimming instead.
Chooses Africa, alone, instead of Brazil, married.

No miscarriage. She's a grandmother who shows photos.
Her million-dollar-heiress-aunt thinks a PhD is a good investment.

He avoids the Columbia-route home. She never lives in Ashland.
The quarter-century Solstice trip ends in Boulder or San Francisco.

The national workshop at Triangle Park has an opening,
so she misses the Lewis & Clark opportunity.

Never attends that TM workshop, consciousness-raising group,
Saturday Class in which Self was encouraged and nourished.

She swims early at Twin Plunges; the tall, handsome man
swims later. Her brother chooses Recovery.

The intricacy and power of small and large choices;
we arrive somewhere important — lonely, intransigent, afraid.

Accidental choosing, little dreams, a powerful stranger —
these propel us forward, create our Dance and fill the Dance Card.

This is assuredly the way I sounded speaking Portuguese after six weeks of language instruction.

INSTRUCTION

BOOKS WE ALL NEED

How to sing in tune,
find a used tuxedo,
find 'cheap eats,'
get to the Rose City.

How to find a real French croissant,
be a *Girl* like Jamaica Kincaid,
floss, polish, iron,
de-clutter a room
        (hint: have a basement or a garage sale)

How to clean wood floors.
pull a rabbit out of a hat,
contact your birth-mother,
glance sideways.

How to find the Public Rest Rooms,
beat the escalator to the third floor,
print,
read illegible handwriting.

How to find your lost love or
        your former High School English teacher,
wreak vengeance,
prepare broccoli,
make a compost pile.

How to understand forsythia,
recover your faith,
choose a single-malt Scotch Whiskey,
start a fan club.

How to become courageous.
How to get up again.

FRIEND OF WRITING

The empty page
is a place of solace and power.
Your words,
their order, and message
can be anything you choose.
They become unstoppable.
A workshop is a safe place to be heard
and to listen.
You will discover that
writing is a chance to love,
to tell the truth, to disagree,
to forgive, to imagine —
and, if you get really good,
to "cook up," in words,
the most delicious meal you've ever eaten.

The best writing has no lace, Walt Whitman wrote.
Franz Kafka noted, *Writing is a form of prayer.*
The six rules of writing:
Read, read, read. Write, write, write.

INSTRUCTION

Eckhart Tolle writes,
There is a stillness
at the center of every moment of Now,
even if we do not notice it.
I do not notice this.
He writes as well, *the locomotive of thought*
keeps us from experiencing
the stillness:
if it were not there,
we would descend into madness.
The mad world would see to it.
After holding my breath
for as long as it's taken
to write these lines,
I exhale, venture to see
if I can touch the stillness.
Near its cusp, but not quite
still.

HOLINESS AND THE DAILY ROUND

A friend is living in the rural southwest — dry landscape, prickly, thorny plants — and poverty, says a mutual friend. Not a get-away like Ashland or Sisters, more like moving out beyond Lakeview, moving to Glide or Hebo. What is the draw of so-far-away? I understand some of what she seeks. I think of Thomas Merton's Holiness and the Daily Round, and deconstruct my own far-away life, calendar filled with meetings and phone call moments. Is there holiness in the headlines, in checking in with Ask Amy, with the "turning on" sound of the laptop coming to life, with the water routine for the geraniums? I sit across the café table from a student, her beauty a holiness. Whatever assists us into the Now is the holiness we need. I eat an oatmeal cookie, lift my teacup, feel its warmth, move this pen across the page. These words aren't holy, but the little nudge that moves the pen surely is.

PERSISTENT SPIRIT

It's like the Möbius strip of the tragic:
a fishing boat capsizes, three men missing,

and what you hear on your compact disk, the Beatles tune,
Imagine all the people living for today.

It's watching the Dow rise and fall, carrying your economic future,
while you eat toast and an apricot.

It's like the way hope and loss are both four-letter words
but share only the "ohhh" of surprise,

the way the bird song excites the hunter in cats
yet seems to be one with the pear tree's blossoming,

the way words both reveal and conceal,
the way pasta needs only browned butter and sage,

but is also good with carbonara —
the way life is both complicated and simple.

ONCE

—*With thanks to Wendell Berry*

Facts don't interest me
as much as character or heart.
It's the look in your eyes
or your laughter, your voice,
that are my keys to you.
Still I can do a "onceness" list
to rival any poet:
I once constructed a small dam,
collecting field stones
in order to slow a creek,
thus creating a swimming-hole
at my Girl Scout camp.
We were supposed to be napping
or writing letters home, but the sound
of moving water called to me.
I once hitchhiked from Oregon
to San Francisco. The first driver
who stopped had the AC on
 "Extremely Cold" in the van.
As we talked I realized
it was a hearse delivering a body
to a morgue in Sacramento.
On the same journey,
a tractor-trailer picked me up at
the rest stop and we raced
toward the "Y" junction
trying to find the hearse:
I'd left my purse on the passenger-side floor.
It held the remaining money—$500—
from my ten thousand-mile cross-country trip.
I lived in a tipi once.

My mother-in-law hasn't spoken to me
for 30 years, since our first meeting.
Some might consider this silence
a stroke of luck.
Last week she told her son,
Tell the wife hello!
My younger brother died on the streets of Baltimore,
homeless, a John Doe.
I picked up his ashes at the P.O.
and walked him home.
Once I cheated on an Algebra test.
I wasn't ejected from the Honor Society,
but I should have been.
The teacher caught-my-eye
and didn't say a word.
He didn't have to:
I still carry that shame,
the disappointment in his eyes.
Recently on a road trip,
I was called *a princess.*
I put my thumb out on Interstate 80
attempting to hitch to Rock Springs WY.
No one picked me up —
an elder carrying a black leather handbag.
The billboards said *Trust In Jesus*
and *If You Die Today Where Will You Go?*
Not one driver was a Good Samaritan.
I used to be so mesmerized by process
that I couldn't get to the content.
In life, I read recently,
it's not so important what you know,
but the ways in which you put it all together.

CANYON

Water and rock
shaped by and shaping each other,
the ultimate composers of landscape.
A woman has climbed from the river's edge,
an alien set down in Eden
before it was covered with green,
before the apple tree.

Notice the sand bars
on alternating banks.
How water pools there,
slow and deep enough for bathing,
while mid-river,
the current ripples move urgently.

The canyon's exposure is layered,
rocks deposited long before
the Holocene,
rocks still eroding
with spring rain and run-off.

The river's gradient, downhill toward Lake Mead,
where it will mirror the sky
above Hoover Dam.

WILD DAYS! WILD DAYS!

Post-modernism is a term that has always bothered me.

Mary Oliver also says, *All my life I have loved more than one thing.* She goes on to add women and men, equally with the trees and dogs, the roses of August and the ponds. And I would add, the cats, and memories of my grandparents, Tom and Nana, and Aunt Anne, my Dad, and especially my Mother, and circles and circles of writers, but at this moment especially each of you. I also love my friends who paint furniture and quilt and knit, and the houses loved by my friends, and some houses loved by people I don't know, and picture books, poetry books, and all of Virginia Woolf's books, especially *To The Lighthouse.* And, in order this morning, waking up, the blue sky's promise, the news report of the $23,000 check, that first cup of coffee I was still drinking when the writers arrived, the washing machine that works, and the confident calls of geese. I, too, love more than one thing, and love living best. Emily Dickinson has a famous first line, *Wild Nights, Wild Nights* and I want to include, *Wild Days, Wild Days.*

WITNESS

— A response to Amy Udell's portraits

Out there in Linn County,
rural, wishing they lived in a Red State,
a high school girl
works with pen and ink,
with graphite on soft white paper,
pays attention to more
than hot cars and the next midnight party
at the quarry along the river.
She's been drawing for years now,
letting her eyes focus and feast
on the details—
how hair curls close to the scalp,
how scarf-fringe unravels,
how eyes separated by a nose
don't exactly match.
Working from photographs,
she has discovered what Johnny is saying,
hands in his mouth, swallowing his hope,
and just how an older child can carry
another child on her back,
both looking up at a stranger with a camera.
Whatever they say, dear Amy,
keep on with your witness,
hand connected to eyes and heart.
Remind us we should pay attention.

ADVICE

Be patient with whatever comes, says Horace, sounding a lot like the Buddha, sounding a lot like Eckhart Tolle. And when you're out there sitting on a rock listening to water, it's pretty easy to follow those instructions. When you brother dies on the street, patience doesn't come to mind, nor does the concept of *enoughness* or abundance. Unexpected death, even predictable and long awaited passing, is like an arrow striking the heart, a wound, really, the size and shape of not-enoughness.

The truth remains that we are, each of us, walking through time. There will never be enough Gypsy Soup or gingerbread, not enough second-hand shops filled with aprons. We'll never discover enough of our own hand-written wisdom about finite abundance. If this were my last day, I'd never want to see the end of the sunset, might even go to Walmart to avoid the serenade of yellow light turning toward darkness.

I close my eyes in this sun-bright space. I am neither light nor frolicsome. I count heartbeats and think about the stamp-sized landscape, trying not to ask for answers.

READING

As you read,
Denise Levertov reminds us,
the sea is turning its dark pages
and up comes, in memory
a Wallace Stevens poem,
The house is quiet and the night is still,
and another poetic line,
She is there at her desk
a bare-bulb illuminating
the page, the side of her face.
I am reminded of so many
hours and days and years,
doing homework at the built-in desk,
typing letters on an old Underwood,
working in Room 203, South Hall
studying *Janson's Art History*,
falling in love with Rilke's
Letters to God,
and Paul Tillich's philosophy
in *The Courage to Be.*
So many desks,
so many years turning pages.
From my reading I discovered
the heart's geography and the words
to say to you,
what Scott Momaday says
in a praise song to the natural world:
You see I am alive, I am alive, I am alive.

THE WOMEN'S ROOM

Fix me, she tells her therapist, *forget the process, the pauses, the small steps forward, the inevitable denial. I need fixing now.* The listening group members laugh aloud, but in their hearts feel the same way. *We're tired,* they think, *we've been at this for years*—since that husband first started cheating, since the children left the nest, bound for college with self-confidence and youthful vigor supplied, cellularly, by each of the older women, each with graying hair.

Next the sibling issues about inherited objects, property and money. The rivalries never seem to end, the elder brother quite sure he has been left in charge of the estate, the younger one pouting and refusing to be present at any meeting that requires him to leave his home. And, unbelievably, unexpectedly, the cousins, first and second, (there was a huge pot of money) and the Church—has something been promised? Is it in writing? It is the woman's job to figure it out, alpha to zed.

Each of them, to a soul, has become a taxi driver, chief negotiator, guardian angel, health care professional, interpreter of law, and prescription drugs. Each still responsible for everything that happens in their nuclear family and the extended family, in and out of state as — Christmas decorations and newsletters, for shopping, for every meal. Maybe a kind husband helps with the dishes, mows the lawn. Everything else is the wife's purview. Some even handle the investments. All of them navigate Medicare, parts A, B. C. and D, Blue Cross too, and because they are utterly responsible, have been to the lawyer to finalize a Will and fill out the "Right to Die" documents—in duplicate.

A therapy group where tea was served became a requirement! These women don't just need a secretary or a room-of-one's-own, they need a life-of-one's-own and a small one-bedroom condo in which to enjoy it.

AFTER CROSSING A SERIES OF OCEANS

I arrive in Liverpool,
a dismal town in November and
not all that much better in the summer.
Perpetual rain, say the prognosticators.
Cold and damp, dressed to hide
the American-ness in me:
Tartan plaid wool jacket,
wool slacks instead of jeans,
my Dad's leather satchel from WWII
instead of a back-pack.
Still, when drivers pick me up,
the first thing they say is,
Where are you from in America?
I hitch north and east into Scotland,
visit the utopian community, Findhorn,
where I pick organic crops for
the dinners we eat, and offer a class
in dance therapy, another on journal writing.
At twenty-five I believe
I can do anything I've experienced.
Findhorn had been founded in the early sixties
by two Hippie Brits in their fifties.
I read about the place in some magazine,
wanted to see the gardens and visit.
They welcome visitors,
though there are few in November.
I stay a week, then head further
north to the Shetland Islands,
then the Hebrides.
I've always loved islands
because there's an end to them.
You can only journey so far,
then you must return or settle down near water.
Thanksgiving, nobody in the world

knows where I am. And where I am
is on a ferry traveling to the mainland,
vomiting in the loo.
Back on terra firma I hitch along the
western coast. My ride is
a lorry driver who's been drinking.
This worries me for several reasons,
so I step out at a secluded intersection
before the sun sets.
Just as I am beginning to wonder
where I will sleep,
an older couple stops.
When they hear my story they say,
We're taking you home for the weekend.
And so I stay with Eleanor and Jack
for two days and three nights before
they drive me to an intersection with traffic.
Indeed, it is a round-about,
so I have several choices about how to head south.
Back in Liverpool, I meet an Australian rugby player
who wants to hitch with me.
We end up in a grain lorry:
an Aussie, an American, a Scotsman
who, hilariously, shout above the engine noise,
and can barely understand each other.
We ride south and then due east
onto the Isle of Skye,
where we play darts and drink a pint
at the only local saloon.
Upstairs is the single B & B in the village.
We stay the night,
and hitchhike back to Liverpool the next day
so I can cross another sea,
a cruise ship headed to the Canary Islands.

THE WRITER'S DESK

On the wall her desk faces,
a small collection of
inspiring visual texts,
among them a pencil sketch —
three trees, new leaves for spring.
A few grasses surround them.
The largest trunk reveals
brown bark coloration.
She purchased the drawing in the
early 70's in southern Oregon, at a
holiday arts and crafts show.
Her friend charged, maybe, twenty-five dollars,
the first work of art she bought.
Beside *Norman's Trees*
a small black-and-white photograph,
an elderly man practices his letters,

     a a a a a a a a

across the right side of a copybook.
His right hand holds an ink pen,
the kind you dip into a bottle, and
his hands give-away his elder status.
This is where all writing begins —
long before the practice-er has any
idea she will send letters to her mother
from Camp Pine Grove, keep a journal,
write poems.

Above the writer, an angel
with a big bow on her head,
found when she cleaned
the Arts Center kitchen last fall.
Then a small handcrafted box with
a right eye looking out at her.

The final piece, a print
of diagonal strips and stripes reads:
Changes Urged in Intelligence.
If none of these work,
she simply opens *365 Tao Meditations*
which advises:
Anything is a subject for a poem.

RETIREMENT

Steve arrives at the table, comparing brain surgery to plumbing. Already we've chuckled through a report from the Brazilian outback and an unpredictable-with-strangers L.A. Thanksgiving dinner. We gather, four writing friends in our sixties, graying hair, brown salt and pepper to silver, all of us with the expectation of dying in the next whatever number of years from one ailment or another. Still it's good to be reminded that any of us might die tomorrow, a bicycle accident, a fall. We're baby boomers who remember the 1960's, recycling, *Ozzie and Harriet*, Jack Kennedy, the Viet Nam War.

It's autumn, too, just as we enjoy the autumns of our lives. Why retirement is good: you can sleep until you damned well want to arise, leave town without a babysitter to orient and pay, get on a flight to Las Vegas or Santa Fe, sign up for a six-week cruise to Greenland or Maui. Sadly, however active you are, you must count calories. OTOH, no one cares if you're a few pounds over your ideal weight. Fifteen is a sweet memory, polished and idealized by decades of the regrettable, the confounding, the mysterious.

So many people have moved into and out of your life that you're not suicidal when one unequivocally says, *So long.* or *Have a good life.* You can visit your children occasionally or everyday, depending, and take care of grandchildren whenever asked or not at all. You know what your budget is, and if you've planned, when the IRAs kick in. Even the news holds no surprises: a Presidential candidate with sex scandals, a secretary who absconds with 42K, a college prof who heads to Mexico with a undergrad. You've seen it all before — tragic for the individual, gossip for the rest. You can make love whenever you want, as long as you don't frighten the cats. It's a fine time, whether you're joyfully single or happily partnered.

PORTALS

Pulled away from the patience of ordinary things,
the tea kettle, the Howard clock, the maple trees in autumn,

I take on the great emptiness, drawer by drawer,
the great letting-go of the unnecessary.

Tomorrow there will be more of the same,
that 1960's skepticism, inbred caution, incessant busyness,

chasing the next deep breath. The mystics say
there are six portals of the senses, the dominant one,

these thoughts like clouds, like a debris-flow
headed downhill toward water.

I hold back at first, a cautious dreamer,
a lapsed Catholic still counting sins.

But if listening can reveal a poem, surely I can tell my friends
from my adversaries, myself from my disguise.

At the altar, divine light shadows walls that whisper,
a vase of hydrangea sits beside one more empty page.

It's a fan with a blade missing, a kite minus a string,
a night light missing the night or a bulb.

A KITE
MINUS A STRING

OTHER LIVES OF THE POETS

Every poet's story begins somewhere.

Mary Oliver wore a black eye patch
to strengthen her lazy eye
and became a careful woods walker.

Linda Pastan grew up in the suburbs of Gary,
and imagined exotic lives for herself
beginning at age ten.

Gary Snyder lived near a Brooklyn bus stop,
longed for trees and isolated hills,
for places no vehicle would ever traverse.

Sherman Alexie lived between the Spokane Rez
and the community college, quit every school
he attended just before graduation.

Billy Collins' dad sold encyclopedias door-to-door
then worked community TV
as a stand-up comic.

William Stafford grew up in Green Acres.
He hated books and school rooms, avoided the library,
wanted to be a bomber pilot like his brother Bob.

Emily Dickinson was a Civil War party-girl,
gossiped non-stop about all her friends,
and thought poetry was for the birds.

Walt Whitman carried a big secret to his grave:
He collected antiques, bought fine suits made in Paris,
and loved the girls.

Edith Sitwell was a kleptomaniac
jailed twice for stealing from her own sister.
That *Dame* business was a fabrication, too.

Even Sylvia Beach, the Paris book store owner,
a fraud who grew up in Garden City,
made herself an exotic ex-pat.

MILESTONES

For my birthday, 62 small, smooth stones from the Hudson River.

On the bathroom windowsill, stones piled two-by-two.

The geologist has labeled boxes of rocks in the basement.

Friend Beatrice gives him stones she cannot identify, followed by long email conversations about their origins.

Long-ago love keeps only the stones I've sent;
everything else is evidence like plutonium.

At the Dunes Recreation Area, the leader gives us hand lenses,
asks *Where do you think this sand originated*?

The longest stone-arch bridge in the USA crosses
the Susquehanna River at Rockville.

On my time line, 1968 was marked by milestones:
graduation, wedding, Peace Corps training, Brazil.

THIS IS JUST TO SAY

I have eaten
the raspberries,
the Wheat Thins
and the string cheese.

I hope you weren't
saving them,
or that last bottle
of Kings Valley Pinot Gris.

Forgive me.
I was up until 2:30 a.m.
writing poems,
doing my homework.

TUESDAY REVELATIONS

Startled by darkness, a dream trails along
toward light. Over coffee, a friend whispers she was
a member of the Church of Pilgrim Holiness.

In Bill's studio – farewell to *Large Woodland*,
welcome, *Tyee Wetland*.
Then Harvest Bisque and crusty artisan bread.

A friend's hand trembles as she speaks about her son.
Later we laugh and share Peace Corps stories stranger
than fiction. Cathy brings roses. Molly brings Emmett.

Kay leaves a volume about Woolf. On the desk of shadows,
shards, and trash, she knows there is a question:
If dusk is a train that passes, what is night?

TRAIN GOING NORTH

Pale skies, westerly winds, Pacific breakers from a two-day storm,
rain clouds stacked against the Laguna Hills, I ride in Business Class.

Car rhythmically sways at 50 mph. San Miguel, Santa Ana, Anaheim.
Red tile roofs, skylights, Winnebago & camper storage.

Off-shore oil wells, harbor seals, bull kelp, waves break into lacy surf.
Sedimentary rock angled to reveal the off-shore subduction zone.

A wild boar scrambles uphill, a '60s white station wagon heads south.
Raptors soar. High in a dry canyon, ranch house with vistas.

Montecito palaces, fields of spinach and lettuce,
trailer outpost for the field workers enclosed by electric fencing.

Delicious solitude. Nobody's off the grid. Airstreams circle the barbeque.
Highway 1 snakes along, approaching, then disappearing from view.

Cattle run from the train's warning whistle —
fields of wild mustard, a nuclear reactor, a prison.

READING EMILY

To venerate the simple days,
is what all writers do —
the ordinary made sacred,
the moment, an epiphany.
The hour precious and limitless.
The morning an invitation,
the afternoon a prayer of gratitude,
the night such an *Ohhh!*
Emily used the exclamation mark
to make her points more than declarative!
— the dash, so the reader would consider
a pause for breath, for wondering and wandering,
so the existential could register on the cerebral cortex,
so that now could be Now.
Of her 1,775 poems, two-thirds mention Truth or Death,
so we know she was keenly aware
that we have a short time to be honest in the world.
Short, that is, when compared to rocks and stars.
Did she also realize that *we are stardust, we are golden,*
and we've got to get ourselves back to the garden?
All writers must arrive at these understandings.
Mary Oliver asking,
What will you do with your one wild and precious life?
Rumi suggesting that we follow his wishes.
Jesus saying, *This is my body.*
Sappho reminding, *They will not forget us.*
Emily realized. *Yes!*
And so do we.

Georgia O'Keefe's eighty foot long painting of clouds in a blue sky

CLOUDS IN
A BLUE SKY

BORN IN PENNSYLVANIA

—pattern from a poem by Charles Thielman

Some days I am the Susquehanna,
slow-moving, green-gray,
headed to the Chesapeake.
Other days I am sheets of rain,
pressed by wind, bending spring grasses.
My genes are coded as fieldstone,
White Pine tracery imprinted on my lungs.
I am accustomed to
an ever-changing sky.

CONVERSATION WITH A POTTER

It was the 70's. I lived in the country
in a refurbished hay barn.
With my grandmother's inheritance,
I purchased a wood stove,
a monoprint by my friend, the art teacher,
a copper kettle.
My neighbor on Frankhill Road was a potter
who threw beautiful bowls and teapots,
complete sets of dinnerware with soft blue glazes.
Always attracted to artists and musicians, I admired his work.
One afternoon as I watched appreciatively,
he looked up from the circling wheel, smiling,
and said without a moment's thought:
But you are an artist too, Ann.
Every day. Look at how you live.

REASONS FOR LOVING POST CARDS

Because they require postage stamps.
Because, in the mail, they are a surprise.
Because someone else can send them, too.
Because they are mailed from far away, even exotic places.
Because the skies are always blue, the sunsets magenta
(It might be heaven).
Because they are all the same size.
Because they don't require an envelope.
Because they begin with a salutation —
Dear Ann — and end with *love*.

THE 19TH HOLE

—Marysville Public Golf Course

At tee-off time for Jeff and Jerry, the ball machine is stuck.
Steve's working the pro shop.
Golfers arrive for a beer, Doritos.
I settle in with a glass of wine & crackers.
There is talk about fishing, the upcoming tournaments:
Seniors, Y-Adults, Youth (8 – 17 years).
An eagle sits atop the Cold Beer refrigerator
and below the Michelob mirror.
Someone told me the first golf balls, before Titleist,
were packed with feathers and leather.
Mondays, $2 Off On Nine Holes.
Rick, a tree-feller from Alsea, talks about early golfer,
Mo Norman, who turned to a couple of guys giving him guff
and announced, *It's going in!* His 210-yard drive did just that.
John and Gary sit at the bar for an Inversion IPA
and some salted peanuts, talk hunting out on Honeygrove Road—
branch bulls running the herd—
and eat packages of oatmeal cookies before a round at 4:30.
Now everyone is telling stories about guys who drink
on the course and then lose it all.
All of a sudden he went downhill!

LOVES' ALPHABET

—Name one thing you love, says Steve

Apples (Liberty) and Ace,
bed-time, boxers – the shorts and the dog,
the cats, old cars, Chapter emails & Courtney.
Several Davids, dusting, D.C.

Errands (crossing-off the list) and my editor,
fabric stores (specialty ones like Pendleton,
or run-of-the-mill stores, like Joanne's),
and friends — life-long like Kathy & CSue
or brand-new, like Bob, whom I met yesterday.

Granola, giraffes, and gingerbread,
hot dogs (with mustard and a baseball game)
icicles, Ian — and jam.

Knitting needles set up with angora yarn,
lemons and lemonade.
Music and maple leaves tinged with frost.
NPR all the time, my niece, my nephew,
and 8th Street neighbors.
River otters (maybe in my next life),
Progress Elementary, the PEACE sign, the Post Office.

The quick and the quixotic.
The Romantics, a romantic, any river.
Nighttime stars and sky, soap-suds, SR.
Tomatoes in late August, Thanksgiving,
the unflappable,
Valentines on any day.

White wine and writing.

There must be something besides *xylophone*
an unwelcome noise — maybe
a flower or bird, a scientific name!
Xanthippe (I'll let you look that up)
and yellow.

Zurich, indeed
all of Switzerland — in any season.

THE TRIBE

The book table is stacked — hundreds of small collections:
Marrow, What the Alder Told Me, Cinders of My Better Angels.

Inside a few lunch-ers sit at round tables,
talking form, talking meter.

A former Corvallian, Greg, of Russian descent,
writes in spring sunshine beside me.

David, channeling Walt Whitman, and his wife
Scottie, arrive for the day.

Steve heads out for a walk; Rachel talks with a Seattle publisher.
The sky is blue, the sun piercing.

I purchase a copy of *Wing Nut* held together with same.
It's for my husband, home with the lawnmower and the cats.

Eleanor gives a tribute to Virginia Corrie-Cozart
dying at home of inoperable cancer.

All writing is collaborative, the speaker said.
The woman beside me says, *My mother smoked four packs a day.*

A small plane chugs along, invisible in the sky.
I say, *I love paying attention to the process.*

THINGS I KNOW

I was a brunette for years and years, for decades before silver hair,
before I looked like my grandmother.

I remember my mother — vividly — as though she were still alive.
I address her often, knowing what would interest her.

Sometimes she appears in dreams, delivering important messages
I can't interpret or forget when I awaken.

My dad doesn't appear in dreams at all, though he outlived her
by eight years, married three months after her death.

He phoned from Florida. I could feel him smiling long-distance,
and was happy that he was happy.

Across the intersection, our neighbors had both the first TV set
and the only swimming pool.

Mr. Zirilli operated a gas station on Rt. 22. Mrs. Z stayed home.
Their son, Pete, was my brother's best friend.

When Tom died, Pete read the obituary and called long distance.
We've been talking and writing since then.

There is a happiness gene in my family.
Maybe a result of surviving the Depression.

Maybe because my granddad was someone everyone loved.
Or because my Nana loved me best.

Later I became the one with *melancholia*, prone to depression,
a weeper with a kind and forgiving heart.

I have been lucky in love. Had a series of wonderful men in my life
— some entirely missing now, some rediscovered.

I suspect that I'll go on talking to strangers and falling in love
right to the end, of this poem and my life.

THE NIGHT SKY

Invisible from sunrise to sunset
veiled by light and the day's activity,
you forget its comforting and infinite calm
as you drive the Interstate, iron,
check the retirement account.

You saw it once, at Pismo Beach,
wild stars arcing across midnight blue,
and down along the Rogue it is ink-black
strewn with white confetti,
an indifferent cosmos celebrating itself.

In the long-ago of your father's arms
beyond the porch light's yellow halo,
you looked out across the fairways:
The moon was a cool wink in the surrounding darkness.
You laughed as you said, *Good Night!*

The ancients thought each star
was the soul of an ancestor.
This remains a comforting theory.

SEPTEMBER TOWN

—Fooling around with line breaks

Those yellow.
Leaves and longing and.
Warm-sun cool.
Air blue-skies children.
Returning to packed.
Lunches with apples.
PBJ on white bread.
No chips. Empty.
Blue, lined spiral.
Notebooks with listings.
Books to read to buy.
Order, paying with chore.
Allowance I remember.
The names of every.
Teacher Riegle through.
Johnson and where I.
Sat in each.
Classroom near my best.
Friend Debbie Lee.
Stevens always.

The fireside aquarium with the goldfish
that has leapt into the fire.

THE FIRE

FIRE

—With thanks to Donna Stonecipher

It was like waking at 3 a.m. the fan still circulating nighttime breezes,
May's half moon illuminating the bed where you sleep alone, wanting.

•

It was like the letter arriving from a dear friend in New York who,
even as a teenager, understood everything about love and loss.

•

It was like that stream she'd discovered in a walk away from a
hundred others, cold and clear and filled with sitting rocks.

•

It was like a talisman—the silver ring engraved *Patient,* the holy medal
from Portugal, the gray pearl waiting to be worn with black silk.

LOVE'S TRAVEL

Valley grasses mowed, vultures troll for mice, for voles.
White wisps of clouds move in from the coast.

Powerball at $6 million, We Buy Standing Timber, near Roseburg.
Super 8, Motel 6, Shari's, and The Sleep Inn, Exit 127.

Seven Feathers Casino just off Garden Valley Boulevard,
Love's Travel Shop, lava outcrop rip-rapped for protection.

An Air Force jet from Klamath Falls marks a contrail.
Bonnie sings, *You'll be forever on my mind.*

As the silver Honda meanders along the Umpqua,
remember the summer fire that threatened Ashland.

Heat and smoke, flames visible from Siskiyou Boulevard,
the first of many fires that have blackened the West

since your arrival in the early '70s. A reminder:
Solitude is the scientific method of the human spirit.

AUNT PEARL'S WATERMELON

—Response to a Calyx *cover photo*
by April Dobbins

Her hands cradle the melon
like an infant she might
hold to her breast or
in the way she held Juan,
swaying on his feet
facing the photographer
at the village market
where she comes to sell agave.
5 agave = 1 melon,
a reward for her children
Aguilar, Martina, Juan,
also her unhappy husband,
no longer *simpatico*,
whose eyes have gone dead
except when he has
too much Tequila.
She remembers the back row
barefoot, hopefully tracing the letters,
unable to read the words.
But all this —
an expected life.

THIS IS MY COUNTRY

—From a lecture by Charles Wilkinson

The villages governed themselves.
Ten language groups of 50,000 Siletz
lived from the Chetco River to the Salmon.
Six miles inland, along the Rogue,
a native camp at Tututin.
Visitors arrived by canoe,
talked, ate, danced late into the night,
sounds of the river current filled the air.
The Chinook band named their territory,
"My Place," "The Only Place," "The Heart Place,"
and vowed, *we will not leave this place.*
At the time of making provisions,
the fire for dancing and the smoke
was visible from the sea.

Annie Minor Peterson remembered
when the food was divided with the elders,
the first Salmon Ceremony,
the dancing and the games, and said,
Long years ago, my people
were happy in our own home.
Everyone was buried there.
The stories arose and were told there.
When the miners arrived they took the law
into their own vigilante hands.
When the Rogue River Wars ended,
Tyee John said, *My heart is sick with fighting.*
I will not lay down my arms and go on the reserve.
This is my country.

THE VIGIL

—*Compiled by Ann, lived by all of us*

Fred phones to tell us, *Now.*
Holly weeps and hugs us hard when we arrive.
I keep thinking my brother is here, are Bill's last words to John.
As usual, dog Lizzie curls-up nearby.
That raspy difficult breathing, but *no pain,*
we are promised by the Hospice saint.
The harpist leaves saying,
I've never felt so much love in a room.

In the hallway, the oxygen tank ticks along.
Cathy and I watch a video on her cell—
grandson, age two and a half.
All of us talk quietly now, telling Bill-stories.
John remembers that big fish Bill landed,
Bill and John extracting a triple-barbed fish hook
from John's father's hand decades ago.
Betty curls beside her husband in the hospital bed,
says, *It's okay to go, Bill. We have a strong family,*
and we'll take good care of each other.

For an hour or two we sleep in the living room.
Awakened at 5:15 a.m. to say final words of love:
Courtney says, *There's a new drift boat*
waiting to take you down the river.
I hold my hand on Bill's chest and tell him,
Where you're going you'll find lots of Indian Princesses —
enjoy them until Holly and I get there.
Hunting pal, Roger's text reads, *When it rains*
I'll think of you, campfires, ditches and tarps, too.

Bill passes.
Now we mourn—that ancient form of love.

WINTER BIRDS, WINTER FIRE

—In response to Wax Wings *by Robert Francis*

It's nearly February,
no snow yet,
no berry bushes in the back yard.
The sky is dove gray,
sometimes close and cold as fog,
today, high and vague
offering no comment.
Out back, two brown juncos search the grass,
alight on the pear tree branches
when I open the door.
If I could hold one in my hand,
I could warm it,
touch tawny feathers,
feel no weight at all:
like my soul
destined for solitude and words,
for winter fire.

THE NEWS

The news of your death comes in the cold light
of earliest spring. Can I breathe?
Moving through dream-shock—
a box of ashes, a box of ashes, white bone slivers,
weight of you, my brother.
I see a homeless man, eyes averted,
shoulders hunched against the light of day,
beaten by the invisible. For your life, Tom,
and my presence in it, I list my mistakes,
all I deny and cannot bear,
not knowing enough to do the next needed thing.
My fear needs its own empty space

compassion and obligation, each a kind of love.
The former requires the latter—a call to action.
Regret. Regret at night before sleep, and every day.
No second chances
unless these words count for something.

LETTER TO A YOUNG POET

Emily said it all,
wisdom revealed in her 1,775 observations
about truth, gardens, fences, the way of water,
friendship.
All the while living in her upstairs room,
slipping down for tea sometimes,
tying little packets of poems together,
an early death.
It was her sister who sent them
to a publisher Emily corresponded with—
the rest is history.
Miss Dickinson was writing
in the same decades as Walt Whitman.
Did she know of him? Read him?
Perhaps her letters say.
She wrote several letters a day,
leaving a trail of hints and clues
about her process, her lack of self-confidence,
sometimes Faith.
So I tell you, dear friend,
I try to do the same.
From my small room,
I slip messages and prayers under the door—
for you, for you.

WITH THANKS TO EMILY

I felt this richness, the world would give and give.
—William Stafford, A Way Of Writing

1.

A slash of blue, and I think of that painting by Carl Morris, of the whole series of "Earth From Above" photographs, the ones my husband and I are looking at day by day — today, skaters at the ice rink in Central Park. *Slash of blue,* and I think of all painters, their tubes and sticks of color - midnight, navy, azure, cerulean turquoise, French—the choices, the dabs of color that make sky and water, heron wing and dusky twilight, that blue which turns to black during my favorite time of day, day, dissolving upward into night. Blue. Blue. Not forgetting those singers—the wail that is part grief, part ecstasy, the piercing raspy *I have been there* blues chord, the harmonica blues, the saxophone ones, too.

2.

Dust is the only secret, gray, soft, fine-particled. I love to watch the dust motes move in sunlight. They do not fall so much as swim in currents of air. Meditative, relaxing, like that scene from the movie, *American Beauty,* where the young, obsessive photographer shoots a plastic bag blown about in an alley between buildings. In the movie this clip reappears several times, no music, just that bouncing plastic moved by invisible winds which asks the viewer to think about the image, its placement and meaning, about the kind of empty, negative, Zen beauty it represents. If Isabel Allende says writing is circular, I'd like to amend her definition to say, *Writing is circular, and it circles the great emptiness,* the mystery of Never again. Never again.

FINDING OUT ABOUT THE LOVE OF GOD

The world is dark now, threatening.
You wonder how you can live through
    this grief, this emptiness.
You no longer notice color,
cannot taste what is bitter or sweet.
The ending goes on and on.
You understand, now, why a person would kill herself,
put rocks in her pockets, walk into the river.
You can no longer remember your favorite song, favorite wine,
where the red suitcase is stored.
The hour-hand on your watch is frozen.
It is always 3 am or 3 pm—the waiting time.
You dream of white-walled rooms, empty, without doors.
Your family is missing; your friends have said their good-byes.
This is when you turn toward God.
Once-rejected, now only He remains.
You might be on your knees.
You remember to breathe and address Him,
hoping for His answer — His love for you.

MAGIC

I see it as an altar, of course, the divine light that fills a writer's room, shadowing cobalt walls, the acorn colored nave where you will go for a discussion afterward. Green tulip stems fill the clear-glass vase; April blooms of coral, red and white tulips. The book is open where you left it after the last meal, open and filled with prose — Faulkner's compulsive voices or Cather's Nebraska praise song, De Lillo's fragmented white noise, Marquez explaining the first decades of his life. Their voices become your own in the galactic magic of the written word, in a room where you've forgotten to light the candles or to touch the lonely fork. Whatever is outside this room, whatever is dire, flooded, extinguished, transfigured, is made whole again at the table.

Why I Write

I write to remember, and because a wise person noted that *writers live life twice* because they write it down. I write because it focuses my thinking, slows it down, because I'm comfortable with a pen in my hand. I write because the past is not past, though I also write so I can consider the future.

I write because it's "the other half" of reading, and so I can talk with those who have disappeared because of death or some other choosing. I write because it can bring on the other half of the correspondence, because I like pens and stationary and stamps. I write to support the Post Office. I write so I can consider my dreams, catch them, analyze them.

I like to write before I speak or listen to others' ideas so I can figure out what I think about roses, horseback riding, or baseball. I learned about this kind of writing and about metacognition at Bard College

I write because I'm not a specialist but a left-handed teacher with a predilection for the under-dog. I write because I no longer believe in god, though I continue to be hopeful about a hereafter where I might talk again with my mother, brother, grandparents, Aunt Anne. I write because it's faster than driving, doesn't require money, often includes a glass of wine, and because, like Willie Nelson, when I started counting my blessings my whole life turned around.

—Ann Staley

CPSIA information can be obtained
at www.ICGtesting.com
Printed in the USA
FSOW01n0631010515
6848FS

9 781620 151853